Cougars For Kids

Amazing Animal Books For Young Readers

**By
Rachel Smith**

Mendon Cottage Books

JD-Biz Publishing

Download Free Books!
http://MendonCottageBooks.com

All Rights Reserved.

No part of this publication may be reproduced in any form or by any means, including scanning, photocopying, or otherwise without prior written permission from JD-Biz Corp

Copyright © 2015. All Images Licensed by Fotolia and 123RF.

[Amazing Animal Book Series](#)

Download Free Books!
http://MendonCottageBooks.com

Table of Contents

Introduction 4

What is a cougar? 5

How do cougars act? 9

What kinds of cougars are there? 15

The history of cougars and humans 17

Cougars and conservation 21

Hybrids of cougars 24

Conclusion 26

Author Bio 27

Publisher 33

Introduction

Cougars, also known as mountain lions, are probably one of the best known local predators in the places like the United States of America. As one of the very few big cats in North America, the cougar sort of inhabits a special place in American and other cultures.

It has no special markings; it's mostly its size that sets it apart from other cats for those who live around it. The cougar is not necessarily loved where it lives, but certainly fulfills an important part of its ecosystem.

What is a cougar?

A cougar is the Puma Concolor, by its scientific name. It's been called mountain lion, puma, panther, and catamount, among other names. It is a large felid, meaning a sort of cat. It actually holds the record for the largest number of names for one animal.

A particularly reddish cougar.

However, the special and interesting thing about the cougar is that it isn't a 'big cat.' This means not that it's not large, but rather that it doesn't belong to the same family as the biggest cats in the world: the lion, the tiger, the leopard, and of course, the jaguar, the only member of the group that lives in the Americas.

Instead, the cougar is related to small cats. This includes the house cat. It is far more closely related to your little pet cat than it is to the jaguar. It's the largest of the small cats, though calling it a small cat seems a stretch of the imagination.

The cougar probably has the widest range of any land mammal. Its range stretches from up in North America to down in South America; it very much lives on both continents, though a lot has been done in parts of North America to clear it out.

How it arrived in America is up for debate, as is when. Cats don't tend to leave fossils so much, for whatever reason, so we don't have much to go on. We do know that its part of the world has never held all that many big cats at all.

The cougar is most closely related to the jaguarundi. The jaguarundi is not related to the jaguar, despite the similar names; instead, it is a small cat about a tenth the size of the cougar. It is spread over Central and South America, though definitely not present in the United States of America. It is also called the eyra cat.

Both of these animals are in the same group, Puma. This makes them somewhat related to the cheetah, but how exactly has not been completely determined.

Basically, the background of the cougar is a bit of a mystery to zoologists and other scientists.

The cougar is very slender and agile; it is the fourth largest cat in the world. They tend to be anywhere from six to eight feet long, though the males are generally bigger than the females.

Interestingly, the closer the cougar is to the equator, an imaginary line that wraps around the middle of the Earth, the smaller it tends to be. It also tends to be bigger the closer it is to the poles, though that is obvious by the previous sentence.

Cougars have five retractable claws on their front paws, and on their back paws, they only have four. Their legs are very powerful, made to seize prey.

Their heads are rounded, and their ears stand erect. They can be as big as jaguars, but in the areas they share territory, they tend to be smaller. Also, even if they are the same size, they aren't built the same; the jaguar is much more muscular.

The cougar is not considered a big cat, despite being one of the largest in the world, for several reasons. One is that it can't roar like the other big cats. It lacks the parts in its throat. Instead, it is best known for its screams.

Sometimes, it's even called for its screams. Its screams are somewhat disturbing, and it often sounds like other animals.

While the color of the cougar is not exactly eye-catching, it can range fairly widely. The cougar, even among siblings, can be anywhere from silvery-gray to reddish. Its natural color is tawny, or brownish.

Some people believe that cougars can be black, confused by the term 'black panther.' But black panther refers to black leopards and jaguars, which are naturally occuring in nature, rather than being a pigment (color) condition like albinism or melanism. There has never been a black cougar that has been documented.

Babies are born with spots. These spots go away when they become adults, though not all at once. Instead, slowly, throughout their adolescence, these spots disappear.

The cougar has large paws, and the biggest hind legs in the cat world. This makes it excellent at leaping and climbing. It can scale things that its canid competitors can't, and this helps to protect it. Cougars are also known to be able to swim, at least to an extent.

How do cougars act?

One thing to know about how cougars hunt is their legs. Like previously mentioned, they have great leaping and climbing ability due to their strong and long legs.

However, unlike their proposed relative the cheetah, they aren't built to run for long. Instead, they do short bursts of energy, and are very fast within that short time frame, but quickly have to stop.

The cougar is a generalist predator. This means it will eat just about anything it can catch, regardless. This ranges from tiny animals to huge hoofed animals.

Cougars are what are called obligate carnivores. This means they absolutely have to have meat. They can't do without, can't substitute something else if they're starving. Obligate is like the word obligated; they have no choice unless they want to starve to death.

Not all carnivores are obligate carnivores, but the cougar definitely is.

Cougars much prefer deer and their relatives; they've even been known to take on bull moose. A full grown male moose is a force to be reckoned with, but the cougar apparently can do that.

They are more likely to hunt white-tailed deer and bighorn sheep, though, than moose.

A cougar stretching.

In some areas, they eat animals such as harbor seals and raccoons too. As stated before, the cougar will eat just about anything it can catch.

The cougar hunts in a specific way most of the time: ambush. It hides in the brush or on ledges or other hidden spots, and then it jumps on the back of its prey. It bites into its neck, and in smaller animals, this can be so powerful it breaks the creature's neck. This bite tends to kill pretty quickly.

After killing a large animal, the cougar tends to drag it away, cover it in brush, and periodically eat it. This takes place over a few days.

The cougar will typically hunt every two weeks. However, a mama cougar may hunt as often as every three days, so she can feed her babies. More mouths to feed, after all.

It has been known to very rarely scavenge, meaning eat the meat of an animal it didn't kill.

Female cougars tend to have a litter of cubs about every two to three years, though they have been known to have them as little as a year apart. A litter typically consists of one to six cubs. Most frequently, it's two.

It's up for debate whether or not cougars are monogamous, meaning they stay with one partner. The belief is that they may instead have several female partners to one male partner. However, it's unknown for certain at this point.

The female is responsible for the cubs. The male does nothing to help. Female cougars are really, really protective of their babies. They've been known to fight even bears off to protect their cubs.

The cubs are not likely to survive in general. Only a little more than one cub on average makes it to adulthood out of the litter.

Cubs are entirely dependent on their mother at birth. They are born blind, and only after three months, after they've been weaned, can they be considered somewhat independent. By six months, they're out of the cave or other home that their mother picked out, and they're learning how to hunt.

A cougar cub will typically learn how to hunt small prey at this age, rather than anything near what its mother hunts.

By two or so, the cub is ready to move out. If the cub is male, it tends to leave younger than if it's female. The further a cub goes from where it was born, the more likely it is that it won't make it. However, it's not entirely certain how this is linked.

Cougars in the wild tend to live about eight to thirteen years; it's thought that they can live much longer in captivity, and there was even a case of a male cougar living all the way to about thirty in captivity.

Why do cougars live so much longer in captivity? The world of a predator is very dependent on being fit. A sick cougar will die quickly; an injured one will too.

If they are just old and can't catch prey anymore, then they will pass on too. If they are old and can't fight other cougars well, then they might be killed by another cougar.

The cougar is solitary. The only time there is a group of cougars is if it's a mother and cubs. Otherwise, cougars only get together to mate.

The range of a cougar's territory is unknown for sure. It seems that males will never let their territories overlap, but females will. Females' territories also tend to be smaller, while males' territories can be enormously huge.

They tend to make their territory by peeing, defecating, and scratching. A cougar can pick up on these signs pretty easily to know that this is not their territory.

The male has harder time getting established than the female when they leave their mother. A male that does not leave their mother's range might be killed by his father. A male generally has to go farther than a female to find a range, and is more likely to be killed by an established male cougar.

Male cougars are very territorial. If they encounter each other, it's likely they will fight. This is only avoided if one backs down.

A problem that has cropped up for these cougars is the relocation efforts of some groups. When you drop unfamiliar cougars into some other cougar's territory, there is going to be a fight. In fact, it makes aggression among cougars far more likely, because the new cougar needs somewhere to stay and is far from home, whereas the current cougar is very certain to defend its territory.

The cougar also makes sounds a lot like a domestic cat, such as purring, chirping, and other noises. This is their way of communicating. Their cubs also make noises not unlike domestic kittens.

What kinds of cougars are there?

Once upon a time, up until about the 1980's, there were about thirty kinds of cougars listed. These are known as subspecies, or small differences between different populations of the same animal.

However, as zoologists have examined these many subspecies, they've discovered a lot of similarities instead, too close to be considered different.

Instead, there are about six. The most notable ones are the North American cougar, which lives in North America, unsurprisingly, and used to be broken up into a lot of different American cougars; the Southern and Northern South American cougars, which are not so different; and the Costa Rican cougar, which is specific to Costa Rica.

However, there is the issue of the Florida panther.

The Florida panther is the presumed cougar that lives in that state. The cougar has been separated from other cougar populations for a long time, and as such, has gained its own characteristics. A lot of people say the Florida cougar is its own species.

A lot of other people say its uniqueness is a result of a lot of inbreeding, and it's still a cougar, simply a subspecies.

A cougar licking its face.

However, its status is currently uncertain in the scientific community. Much of the accepted view is that it's a cougar, and not its own species, but it's not entirely accepted.

The history of cougars and humans

Cougars have long featured in the Native American stories and other parts of their cultures. Which is fair, as it's a powerful, captivating creature, much like wolves, lions, and other creatures are big parts of European folklore.

A cougar lying down.

The cougar was very much celebrated and admired in the Incan empire. The Incas are a people we only know so much about, as most of their culture was destroyed by colonialists. The Spanish invaded, took over the Incan empire, and erased most of their culture, as they did with a lot of peoples.

But, it's said that the capital city of the Incan empire, Cusco, was shaped to look like a cougar. The Incan people also named regions and their children after the cougar. Also, Viracocha, the Inca sky, and thunder god, seems to have been associated with the cougar.

Other groups thought of the cougar differently. In North America, the Winnebago, also known as the 'Ho-Chunk' people, included them in many stories, as did the Cheyenne.

For the Apache and the Walapai, both peoples of Arizona, the scream of a cougar was very bad sign. In fact, they considered it a sign that someone was about to die.

Algonquins and Ojibwe peoples believed that the cougar was wicked. They believed it belonged in the underworld.

On the other hand, the cougar was sacred to the Cherokee.

Nowadays, while most of those peoples still have those stories and those beliefs, to an extent, the biggest focus on cougars by much of the citizens of the countries they live in is the damage they do to livestock.

Cougars will freely hunt livestock. The livestock are very easy prey, because they have been bred to be easier to control. Therefore, a lot of cattle are too dumb to fight back, as are animals such as sheep.

Essentially, humans are mad that cougars have taken advantage of our breeding of livestock to make them easy prey.

The solution to most ranchers was simply to kill off, or hunt, the cougars.

The issue, however, was that this only led to more livestock deaths.

Why? You would think that killing them would mean less livestock deaths. But, the issue is that they were and are killing cougars already settled into their territories, and are typically less likely to attack livestock. When those cougars are cleared out, young, new cougars take their place, and these cougars are far more likely to go after livestock.

So, unless all cougars are completely wiped out for hundreds of miles, this system of remedial hunting is a very bad idea.

And of course, wiping out cougars is also a very bad idea.

Cougar attacks on humans are extremely rare. Within a period of hundred years, there were about fifty attacks in the United States of America. Consider this: millions of people had the opportunity to be attacked. If only fifty out of millions were attacked, then the chances of getting attacked are extremely tiny.

A cougar will typically only attack if it feels cornered by the human, or if it is severely starving. In general, cougars don't recognize humans as prey.

The key with a cougar attack is to do stuff like hit it with a stick and try to scare it away; standing still or playing dead will only make it think the human is an easy target. Playing dead may work with some animals, but not cats.

Usually, there are signs that a cougar will probably attack a human at some point. If they are out during daylight a lot, even though cougars are crepuscular or nocturnal (meaning twilight/dusk and nighttime activity instead of daytime), or if they show no fear of humans, plus stuff like actively stalking humans, they will probably hurt a human.

This is incredibly rare, and a reason that cougars absolutely should not be pets.

The Argentine cougar is described as absolutely not being willing to hurt a human. They will not fight back against hunters. They have been described as even leaving sleeping humans alone, being somewhat afraid of humans.

Whether or not it's true that the Argentine cougar will not harm a human even if it's attacked by one is unproven. It will hopefully remain unproven, because it's a bad idea to attack a giant cat, regardless of its reputation.

Cougars and conservation

Cougars are not endangered. They are considered to be in the category of Least Concern.

The cougar was once nearly hunted out of North America. Pushed out until most of what remained was the cut off Florida panther population.

This was due to the ranchers, who didn't like the way that the cougar attacked their cattle or sheep. Basically, there was a campaign to get rid of the cougar.

It still hasn't come back to much of its old territory. Cougars used to live in places like Ohio, New York, Connecticut... you'd be hard-pressed to find one there now.

It used to live all the way up in Eastern Canada. It does not now.

However, the cougar has revived in a lot of the more Southwestern parts of the United States of America, and is even doing well in a small part of Canada.

It is not a good thing to get rid of a top predator. The cougar provides an important role for the environment, which is keeping the prey populations from getting too big.

If there isn't a predator to curtail the prey population, they will grow too big, eat too much food, whatever their source, and cause problems for the environment. Then, the prey will have to starve until their numbers go down. Then the process starts all over again.

So, predators are needed for control. The predators' population is controlled by the population of the prey, so it balances out nicely if left alone. The issue is that it's not often left alone by humans.

A cougar cub.

In much of its range, such as Bolivia, Colombia, and Honduras, to name three, the cougar is protected. These countries realize that they need the cougar to keep their ecosystems balanced.

However, that is not the case in the United States of America. Instead, about a hundred a year are killed by Americans. To be fair, it is a bit difficult to legally kill a cougar. One must have proven property damage, such as an animal being killed, in order to get a permit. Then, the permit usually allows an American to take his dogs, chase the cougar up a tree, and then shoot it.

Texas, however, is a little easier. Because Texas lists the cougar as nuisance animal, anyone with a hunting permit can kill it. They don't keep track of how many are killed either.

Hybrids of cougars

There is really only one hybrid of a cougar and any other animal: the pumapard. This is a cross between a cougar and a leopard.

A picture of a pumapard in 1904.(Wikimedia Commons)

The poor pumapard is pretty much doomed from birth. They don't live long, due to their parents' poor matchup, and they are almost always dwarves.

A pumapard has particularly short legs, and is about half the size of its parents. It has been described as having a tawny color, in most cases, with brownish rosettes, the spots of the leopard parent.

Back at the turn of the 20th century, or the early 1900s, the idea of crossing cougars and leopards came up. It sounded cool to the people who did such things, and so they did it.

The pumapards were lauded as fascinating creaturs, for the most part, though some described them as boring.

As far as the world is aware, there are no living pumapards.

Conclusion

Cougars are an integral part of the Americas' various ecosystems. We are quite lucky they are still around.

With as interesting a past, and as hopeful a future, as the cougar has, it will continue to be a part of the Americas' cultures, and hopefully live on to be the subject of many more stories.

Author Bio

Rachel Smith is a young author who enjoys animals. Once, she had a rabbit who was very nervous, and chewed through her leash and tried to escape. She's also had several pet mice, who were the funniest little animals to watch. She lives in Ohio with her family and writes in her spare time.

Download Free Books!
http://MendonCottageBooks.com

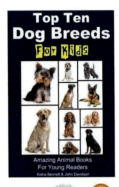

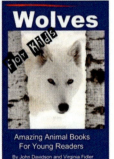

Our books are available at

1. Amazon.com

2. Barnes and Noble

3. Itunes

4. Kobo

5. Smashwords

6. Google Play Books

Download Free Books!
http://MendonCottageBooks.com

Publisher

JD-Biz Corp

P O Box 374

Mendon, Utah 84325

http://www.jd-biz.com/

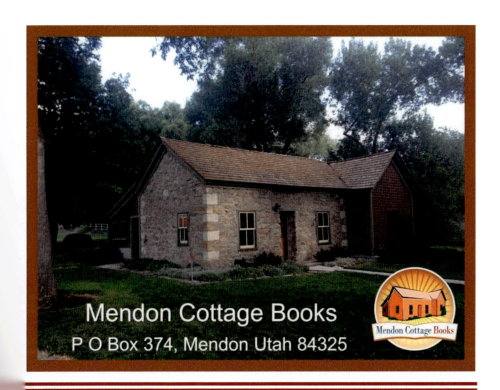

Made in the USA
Monee, IL
08 January 2021